73

How to Love the Empty Air

ᲪᲚ

Poems by Cristin O'Keefe Aptowicz

Write Bloody Publishing
America's Independent Press

Los Angeles, CA

WRITEBLOODY.COM

O'Keefe Aptowicz, Cristin.
1ˢᵗ edition.
ISBN: 978-1938912801

Cover Design by Zoe Norvell
Interior Layout by Winona Leon
Proofread by Sarah Kay
Edited by Wess Mongo Jolley, Sarah Kay, and Derrick C. Brown

Type set in Bergamo from www.theleagueofmoveabletype.com

Printed in California, USA

Write Bloody Publishing
Los Angeles, CA

Support Independent Presses
writebloody.com

To contact the author, send an email to writebloody@gmail.com

MADE IN THE USA

HOW

TO

LOVE

THE

EMPTY

AIR

By Cristin O'Keefe Aptowicz

How to Love the Empty Air

My Mother Does Not Give Advice

to me, at least. Instead she emails inspirational quotes.
Read this from Tao Te Ching, her email says,

> *"Those who know they do not know*
> > *gain wisdom…*
> *those who pretend they know*
> > *remain ignorant."*

And that's great news for you, right?
Because if there is one thing we both know
it's that you have no idea what you're doing!
I'm kidding! she writes before adding
in parentheses, all caps: *I AM NOT KIDDING!!*

My mother is trying. My mother is skittish.
My mother is an uncertain north star.
She knows she guides me, but doesn't like it,
doesn't want to be blamed if everything goes wrong.
Sometimes everything goes wrong.

Never fear shadows… she emails the following week,
they simply mean there's a light shining somewhere.

Did you write that? I asked her. *No*, she says,
copied it. You're the one that writes books, I just read them!
which is only true because she was the one
born in 1950, and I was the one born to her.
She made the world open to me. And now
that my world feels in chaos, I return to her,
ask her to tell me what to do. She won't say it.

Instead she emails articles, essays, quotes, aphorisms,
and today, a parable:
> *"Come to the edge," he said. They said, "We're afraid."*
> *"Come to the edge," he said. And they came.*
> *And he pushed them… and they flew.*

On Trying to Accept That I'm Not Moving Back to NYC

my skyline, my byline, my buzzer and door
now you're the dream we lived before
—Deborah Garrison, from "Goodbye New York"

Goodbye to the subway rides, equal parts
working class pride and early morning dread:
the hole in the street I literally had to crawl
out of to get to work.

Goodbye to the Bowery, who started in my life
so ragged and worn, and who now is as sequined
as a showgirl. I like to think I had zero part
in making you who you are today.

Goodbye to the Neptune Diner, its 24 hour booths,
its lox omelets and thick pancakes, the Greek waiters
whose relentless surliness became a point of pride:
They liked me.

Goodbye NYC parks, Washington and Union Square,
Madison and Tompkins, Central Park in all its gaudiness,
its enormous expansive excess. Goodbye Astoria Park,
the one park I called home.

Goodbye to the museums I never explored, restaurants
I never ate at, places I read about but never visited.
Goodbye top of the Empire State. Goodbye Roosevelt
Island. Goodbye Statue of Liberty, your crown, your torch.

Goodbye zip code. Goodbye area code. Goodbye saying it:
I'm a New Yorker. Feeling its weight. I already miss your
all-night bodega sweepers, your weary taxi drivers,
the bicyclists who tried to kill me every day.

New York City, I want to return to you a better woman, a better writer. Return to you so clean, you won't even recognize me, so glorious, you'll dim your lights, so damn grown that maybe, just maybe, I can look you in the eye.

MOVING MEANS THAT YOU HAVE TO TOUCH EVERYTHING YOU OWN ONCE

Hello, tiny porcelain rabbit
I'm supposed to use as a ring dish.
I'm sorry I own no rings.

Hello, literary journals from high school,
prom dresses from high school, prom
pictures from high school, yearbooks.

Hello, literary journals I'll never read.
Hello, water color portraits of guys
I never even got to kiss.

It's good to see you again, empty CD cases
of CDs I loved. I've missed you, soft hoodie
with the huge ink stain.

Kitchen, you are my favorite. I dump
whole drawers of you into boxes. Even
the ugliest mugs get to hitch a ride.

Bathroom, we will likely be parting ways
with most of you. I apologize, half-used
baby powder. It is not your fault.

The clothes I stuff into garbage bags,
which are easier and cheaper than boxes.
Soon I am left with just the books.

I take a fat black marker and write on three sides
of every heavy box: *Non-Fiction, Non-Fiction,*
Non-Fiction. Memoirs, Memoirs, Memoirs.

Poetry, Poetry, Poetry. I slap labels
and tape, and stack everything in corners,
until finally, I am alone.

My suitcase and my sweat, my shaking hands,
my buzzing teeth. The smashed pair of shoes
by the door just waiting to leave for good.

PORTRAITS OF MY MOTHER, FAR AWAY FROM TEXAS

After we are done with what will be our final hug for a while,
my mother tells me she is going to turn the car around so
I can see how sad she is that I am leaving for Texas.

Mom, I tell her, *I'll be back. It's just for a year. I just need to finish
this book.* But neither of us can help it. She turns the car around,
hangs out her window, dreary as a hound that's lost its sense

of smell. At some point, we start laughing. At some point,
we stop. *Take a picture,* my mother half-jokingly demands,
take a picture with that fancy phone of yours so you can always remember

how sad I was that you left. I take it and make it her contact picture.
Weeks later, she calls as I am wading through another regretful,
sweaty night in Austin. When the phone rings, that photo appears.

I stare at it, at her. It reminds me not to complain. We both wish
I wasn't here, but I am here. I am here. I am here. When I pick up,
my mother and I lie to each other for a while, about how good

it's been since I've moved. Finally my mother gives up the ghost,
says, *I want to say I'm sorry for being so hard on you leaving.* Oh mom,
I tell her, I knew you were joking. *Yeah, but I was thinking. You know,*

I've never lived farther than twenty miles from the neighborhood I grew up in.
I've lived in Philadelphia my whole life. Now Texas wouldn't have been
my first choice, but you are doing something. Striking out on your own.

And I want to say I'm sorry if I made that harder for you. Outside,
the sun refuses to go down. Dead grass sizzles in its orange glow.
Thanks, Mom, I say. Then I tell her about the photo she made me

take, and how when she calls now, it's the picture that pops up.
Oh, don't do that! she says, *That's not the picture I want you to see.*
Use that other one. You know that one, from our weekend together?

So after we hang up, I make the switch. Now when she calls,
I see the version of her she wants: her grinning like a criminal,
barely holding it together, pointing to a huge sign that reads,

It's Nutts!

MIDTOWN

When I lived in New York City,
I'd sometimes walk behind beautiful women
just to watch how men would stare at them.

Afterwards, I'd try to catch the men's eyes,
let them know I saw them, see if they'd be
embarrassed. Most of the time they'd look

right past me. Sometimes I'd work so late
the office lights would shut off around me,
the motion detectors not sensitive enough

to detect the dumb tapping of my keyboard.
So I'd stand up, wave my arms around, jump,
just so the system would know that I existed.

Other times, I was happy to stay in the dark.
In Texas, no one walks. It's too hot. Plus,
there are things called *cars*. Still, I walk.

For months, I walk. The only person I see
is my shadow, this darkness trailing behind me
that I'm unable to shake. Or, depending

on the time of day, and where I find myself
going, an emptiness in front of me
I'm always chasing but can never catch.

LENOX

Omar and I drive from Austin to Philly
in exactly thirty six hours. We stop only
to eat meals at Cracker Barrel and to sleep
in the sketchiest hotel in Georgia.

I make the drive from Philly to Lenox alone,
in just one day, in a pummeling snowstorm.
I arrive exhausted at Taylor's, who has dinner
already prepared. When we both get truffle oil
on our iPhones, he un-ironically says,
Welcome to the Berkshires!

The next morning I drive to Lenox,
to the Clampitt House, another residency
to which I am escaping.

The Clampitt House,
where I'm being given the gift of being paid
to write, to live alone for the first time
for six months. Six months, all mine.

The Clampitt House, where I will finish
the books itching under my skin, where
I will sleep and eat and breathe
under my own watch.

It is where I will start
being who I am supposed to be.

It is where I find out just
who that is.

LENOX II

During my tour of the Clampitt House,
I keep bursting into tears.

The woman from the Arts Council
showing me around just smiles.

I know the last four residents
were men. They probably didn't

start weeping when they saw
the book-strewn kitchen nook,

or the well-used fire place,
or the bright, airy office,

the washing machine and dryer,
the second floor bedroom,

its cozy down bed, its warmth,
its light. *I'm sorry, I'm sorry,*

I keep telling her, unable to keep
myself in check. *No, no,* she says,

You can feel however you like.
Just know that we are so happy

you are here.

My Mother Wants to Know if I'm Dead

ARE YOU DEAD? is the subject line of her email.
The text outlines the numerous ways she thinks
I could have died: slain by an axe-murderer, lifeless
on the side of a highway, choked to death by smoke
since I'm a city girl and likely didn't realize you needed
to open the chimney flue before making a fire (and,
if I do happen to be alive, here's a link to a YouTube
video on fireplace safety that I should watch). Mom
muses about the point of writing this email. If I am
already dead, which is what she suspects, I wouldn't
be able to read it. And if I'm alive, what kind of daughter
am I not to write her own mother to let her know
that I've arrived at my fancy residency, safe and sound,
and then to immediately send pictures of everything,
like I promised her! If this was a crime show, she posits,
the detective might accuse her of sending this email
as a cover up for murder. *How could she be the murderer,*
if she wrote an email to her daughter asking if she was murdered?
her defense lawyers would argue at the trial. In fact,
now that she thinks of it, this email is the perfect alibi
for murdering me. And that is something I should
definitely keep in mind, if I don't write her back
as soon as I have a free goddamn second to spare.

EMPIRE

In the months that follow, I learn
how to zip my dresses by myself.

To press my hip or back against a wall
to hold the fabric in the place

where once a lover would've held me,
and tug the stubborn zipper

until its teeth gnash closed against
every lump and curve.

Has anyone designed a dress
for the lonesome woman?

The zippers could run up the front,
and look like the scar you get

when a surgeon takes out your old heart
in order to replace it.

Everyone would know, of course,
when they see the dress

about the state you've found yourself in,
but doesn't everybody know already?

In my life before,
I wore dresses so rarely.

Now, I put one on every day,
and stare at the woman gritting her teeth

in the mirror, sweaty hand on zipper,
trying to make the impossible possible.

Sometimes I look like a stranger,
a person I never thought I'd be.

Other times, I look like a woman
who is at least trying, like a person

that I am choosing
to become.

Lenox III

I print out all the poems
and make a fire.

I make a fire and sit
in front of it with the poems.

It's all there.
Every awful thing.

Every sign I didn't see.
Everything I didn't want

to admit to myself.
Everything used

and everything wasted,
all bound by the edges

of these small sheets of paper.
All you have to do is

make sense of it all,
I say to myself,

All you have to do
is love it enough not to want

to throw it on that fire.
Remember, nobody is perfect,

the fire tells me,
before she uses up everything

she's been given and
simply collapses into ash.

LENOX IV

On the phone, I tell Ernie
I'm a pragmatist, and I use
the information I am given.

I am thirty-four and unmarried,
therefore I am not the type of woman
who people want to marry.

I am thirty-four and childless,
therefore I am not the type of woman
who is going to be a mother.

I am thirty-four and this nonfiction book
hasn't sold yet, therefore I shouldn't
trust that it ever will.

I'm thirty-four, and I don't know
what I'm doing with my life,
therefore it's reasonable for me

to be this anxious, this uncertain,
to be feeling this unmoored,
my heart cringing in my hand.

And he says, *Yeah, but what if?*
And I say, *But what if what?*
And he says, *But what if*

everything?

MONEY

You know, it's just money.
And what's money, anyway?

Oh yeah, that's right:
It controls fucking everything.

AUSTIN II

The auction is scheduled,
and as it turns out, it will happen
when I'm visiting friends in Austin.

After weeks of talking to editors,
my nonfiction book blushes
on its pedestal, waiting.

My agent tells me to be patient,
but even she didn't think
it would go on for three days.

On the last day, my agent calls me
at Ernie's house to tell me the news.

I hang up the phone
and he comes into the room
and says, *Well…?*
and I say, *My world has changed.*

I smile as my face explodes
with the world's happiest tears.

*I think I think I think
I need to lay down*, I finally tell him.

And he says, *Of course,
but not on the floor. Come lay down
on the bed. I want to hear*

everything.

Austin III

I call my best friend on the phone.
In Philadelphia, watching *Calliou*
with her toddlers, she whispers
into the phone as she walks out
of the room:

I've been waiting for you to call!
What happened? What happened?!

So I tell her what's happened,
she lets out a stream of joyful expletives
with which only a true Philadelphian
could grace the world.

Bernadette, she tells her shocked five-year-old,
who has stumbled into the hallway, *you didn't*
hear what Mommy just said and you aren't going
to hear what she's saying next.

And we scream at each other until we cry.
Do you know why they're paying that much?
she finally asks me.

Oh Lord, I have no earthly idea, I reply, tearfully.

Oh honey, she says, *I know.*
It's because you deserve it.

AUSTIN IV

On the drive to my friends' house,
I tell the sun. I tell the fields.
I tell the huge Texas sky.

I tell my mother,
who I won't actually tell
for another week.

I tell the car. I tell myself again
and again until I believe it.

When I arrive at my friends'
house, they are in the middle
of making dinner: vegetarian
chili and homemade carrot cake.

*We were hoping there would be something
to celebrate*, they say, smiling at me.

I look at them,
still vibrating
with the news of it,
and smile back.

LENOX V

When I come home,
I tell the house.

I tell the fireplace.
I tell the kitchen.

I open the door,
and tell my office.

I tell my research books.
I tell my laptop.

I tell my coffee cups
and thick woolen socks.

I tell Amy Clampitt herself,
smiling in silver frames.

It worked, it worked,
I tell each of them.

We did it. We did it.
Magic is real.

After Telling My Parents Via Skype, My Mother Sends Me an Email

Oh Cristin,
I'm still so thrilled with your phenomenal news! You worked
really hard (<u>really hard!</u>) for this, so it must feel great. Now
I'm glad I saved all your 'precocious scribbles' in the attic…
Can you say *Hello eBay*! I'm kidding! (Or am I?) Anyway,
I have to tell you this story about your dad. So we get off
the video-call with you and Daddy returns a phone call he got.
Some poor paddling acquaintance was the unsuspecting audience.
25 minutes later your Dad is still at it: *Hey, Chuck… I'm an engineer,
a practical guy. I don't know anything about writers. This whole 'book thing'
is a mystery to me. BUT*… and then your father proceeds to detail
every award, every residency, every fellowship and your book auction
and sale… *Hey, Reen, is a publisher the same thing as an editor?* Turns out
all the guy wanted was to remind Bruce to send a check for his share
of their Nags Head rental! The poor guy is 67. He was probably
thinking *Man, my prostate is acting up and I have to pee so bad!* Anyway…
we are both so proud of you! But you know, me more because
I actually know what you are talking about! We'll have to figure
out a way to celebrate soon!
Ma

ON GETTING FACIALS WITH MY MOTHER

We are working class girls, her upbringing even rougher
than mine. But we have reason to celebrate, and decided
to do so together in a hotel and spa in Princeton, NJ.

How about facials? My mom asks, and I say, *Sure,*
choosing the least expensive one. We walk into the spa
a couple nervous terriers, pretending we've done this before.

We listen to the instructions, ask no questions.
Change into gigantic robes. We shuffle plain-faced
in ten dollar flip flops, and drink water with lemon.

When it is time for our facials we are separated.
In the room, Jennifer shines a spotlight on my face,
asks me "my routine," how old I am, if I have any kids.

She slathers my face again and again, shakes my pores
for loose change, tells me I need to moisturize,
that things like the air, the sun, the wind, even my job

does its share of damage. But I listen to only
the first thing she says: to breathe deep, to let go
of everything I brought into the room.

Let go of the naked slim woman in the sauna,
the teen boredly texting through her pedicure,
her tan mother, the $90 dollar moisturizers,

the $125 face washes. That feeling of *does not belong*
that runs its fingers up my back whenever I leave
the neighborhood. But ma and I, we're here nonetheless.

Both of us trying to breathe deep, let go. Somewhere,
years are being erased from my mother's face.
She tells the facialist about me, her daughter,

the writer down the hall. How we don't do stuff like this.
How much we need it. After an hour, we're reunited.
She looks beautiful: stripped down and glowing.

We put on our clothes and yes, we swallow hard
when the cashier gives us the total, but we shake it off.
We wear our new faces right into the sun, just like

we're told not to do. We can't help it.
The air feels too good, the future so bright.

SOMNOLENCE

In my dreams, I'm always trying to wake up.
Usually, it's because I think I'm late for work.

Even now, when writing is my only job, and
I'm a very kind boss, this anxiety plagues me.

Sometimes I'll get out of bed in the middle
of the night and rush to put on pants and shoes,

not noticing the darkness everywhere. In my dreams,
I'm always behind, always forgetting something,

always disappointing someone. But when I wake,
the world shifts: I know who I am and what I have

to do. This is maybe why I am a morning person.
How happy I am to wake in this life I call mine.

10AM WRITING SESSIONS

are on the agenda all week long. I'm on deadline
and it's the last week of my six month residency
in Lenox. My family—my entire family—is vacationing
at the state park just down the highway. The rest
of the family are outdoorsy types. Not mom and me.
So we schedule writing time: 10am until 10:45am,

every day, in her cabin. Someone take these
grandchildren away, we are not to be interrupted!
My mother and I sit across from one another,
with our fresh mugs of coffee and our very
unnatural laptops. This is where I feel most
at home: with her, surrounded by books.

My mother is an indecisive writer: certain of her
talent, certain of the stories she wants to tell, but
impatient with the drafts it takes to get there.
She is a flamboyant procrastinator, wanting to be
caught badly. She plays music, videos, excuses
herself for water, drums her fingers on the desk.

I try to be the model writer in front of her: dedicated,
unwavering, keeping those fingers moving no matter
what. If needed, we brainstorm ideas, confirm that
nothing has to be perfect, that writing is not about
the end product, but the process. That she shouldn't
just write what she knows, but she should write what

she wants to say. This morning, we are both doing well.
The writing is a steady stream, and our coffee mugs
are remaining full and untouched. Tomorrow and
tomorrow and tomorrow we will meet again.
At the end of the week, seven little pieces.
A novella, a collection, a time capsule: *proof*.

On Renting a House an Adult Would Live In

It is too nice. Like a dress I'd admire until I saw
the price tag. But in the video Ernie tells me,
Here is your backyard. Isn't it beautiful? Imagine
your little dogs running around here. It's yours.

Austin, when I left you for Lenox, I never imagined
I'd return. You are so far away from everything and
everyone that once served as my definition of home.
But I find myself happy to be pulled back

into your impossibly sunny arms. As I pack up
in Lenox, Derrick and JB are already filling
these new empty rooms. Anis helps Ernie bring
over the books, and together they all make this

a home. A home I'll live in. A home where
I'll write. A home where I will move forward.
All in this little house that feels too good for me,
with its white bathtub, its little doggie door,

the bedroom that fills every morning with light.
Derrick texts me a picture of my new office,
Your desk awaits you, he texts. I stare at it.
My desk awaits me, I think. That empty air

awaits my words. I await this strange, new future,
the one I love, and never saw coming.

BARTON SPRINGS

When they locked the north gates early,
we decide to just walk across the river bed
in our bare feet, the tallest carrying our towels

on his head. When we reach the springs,
the night is still warm, but so dark. Austin
in late summer, and everyone is laughing.

The water feels like a kiss: all wet and wanted.
Everyone is in love: the moon and the water,
the diving board and the rocks, the night air

and the howls we released into it at midnight.
Weeks ago, you told me you'd never been.
That you felt too pale, too awkward to go.

In the dark, I swim towards you, even though
you aren't here. Still, I swim to you, the hope
of you, under the pale, perfect Texas moon.

STRING THEORY

I can't help but see the lovers walking, how happy
they are and how they don't even seem to know it.

Here, a wife spoons good soup into her husband's
smiling mouth. Here, someone says, *Look at you!*

You've won the love of a beautiful woman! The pair
blushing into each other, shimmering at the table.

Here, sunlight falls on everything that is real.
When you and I fall into each other at night,

we're our own solar system. Everything revolves
around us. Everything spins and flares. Last night,

I held your face, kissed it, and said it out loud
for no one else to hear: *thankyouthankyouthankyou.*

When I said it, I meant it. It felt realer than dirt.
This morning, I hold the memory of us tight,

this small stone I hope to press into a diamond,
but worry, instead, I'll crush into dust.

Preparing for the Hardcover Tour

When we are a thousand miles apart, I will think of you:
how my hands glided across the caps of your shoulders,
your shirt easing down your arms. How I thought, *Christmas*,
as if you were my present. I will remember your head tipped
onto my spine, one hand flat on my neck, the other buried
in my hair, how there was nothing but our breathing in the night.
I will remember after: us on our backs, the sweat like sugar
frosting our bodies, our trembling legs knotted on the sheets.
I will remember leaving. I will remember leaving all those times
when I could have stayed. How I found my way around
your furniture in the dark: shoes, purse, keys, cardigan.
How I snapped off the lights, brought you a glass of cold water.
How surprised you looked. How you pulled me down to thank
me, your lips light and warm. How afterwards, I straightened up
and left. How I left. How I left anyway. How now I wonder
if I'll ever make it back.

ON RETURNING FROM THE HARDCOVER TOUR TO YOU

What is another word for *sweetheart,* for *darling*?
What is another word for **lover**, for *honey*, for *baby*?

Every pet name that could blossom from a pair
of lips, I've already painted on someone else.

Same with you, I know. When you count the rings
in the hacked trunks of our most recent relationships,

my count was eleven; yours, fifteen. So I think
we can be forgiven as we stare at this sapling,

just over a year old and still nameless. I'm sorry
it took so long for me to feel comfortable hugging you

in the kitchen; to not be surprised at your kiss
at the door; to be able to rest my head against

your chest when we watched a movie. *I'm sorry,*
I find myself saying when I stand awkward

in your bedroom, my cold feet, my stumbles,
my clunks, my scuffs. *You never have to apologize,*

you tell me, *you know that, right?* and I say I'm sorry.
I'm sorry I just said I'm sorry. Sorry about that.

I'm sorry I'm still surprised by it all, my love.
It's just feels so new, and I feel so grateful.

Isn't Every Love Poem an Unfinished Love Poem?

Praise the ear.
Praise the hair curling
around the ear.

Praise the music
we never turn on,
only make.

Praise the caps
of your shoulders, my lips
pressed against them.

Praise the poem
I was trying to finish
when you showed up

at my door.

MOTHER'S DAY, 2015

One of the perks of being the one childless kid in the family
is that it means I get Ma all to myself for Mother's Day.
Every year, I fly home to be with her. This year, my mother
is a parade float filled with fireworks. You can see her pride
from outer space. On this trip, she carries two canes, *temporary*,
she assures me. Her body, like mine, always falling apart.
Her body, like mine, always moving forward. We walk together,
as slow as she wants, through Longwood Gardens, through
Delaware diners as shiny as rocket ships, through the parking
lot of a dinner theater production of *Steel Magnolias*. Mom, I say,
the daughter dies in this play. What are you trying to tell me?!
She laughs, a freshly shaken bottle of apple cider. When I return
from the bathroom, all the people at our table know. *Your mother
is very proud of you*, they tell me. *New York Times Best Seller*,
my mother crows as the lights dim, *for three months!* I can see
her smiling in the dark as the actresses storm the stage, cackling.
I worry about what I need to tell her. That the man in my life
has told me he wants to marry me. How I want to marry him too.
That I want to stop my vagabond life of chasing opportunities.
That I want to stay. That I want to stay in Texas, of all places.
My mother and I always have shared one dream: to be a writer.
I'm there now, for both of us. She goes to bookstores, moves
my books to the front table. Goes to libraries, and texts about
how many people are on my book's waiting list. When it made
that best seller list, she was the first person I called. We both
wept into our phones. At my events, she wears bright red jackets,
a homemade pin reading *I am the Author's Mother* fastened
like a medal to her chest. Over manicotti and lasagna the next night,
she asks about what I'm writing next, and it all comes out.
I look up at her finally, and see my mother smiling at me,
her eyebrows raised with surprise. *I am so proud of you*, she tells me,
taking my hand, *you should enjoy what you've worked so hard for.*
And know this, she adds, with a squeeze, *you have earned
every happiness you've got coming to you. Every. Last. One.*

On Never Imagining It Ever Actually Happening

Thank you.

On Never Imagining It Ever Actually Happening II

Fuck You.

To My Mother Whose Body Is Trying to Kill Her

Have you heard the new Janelle Monae song? It's really good.
If you haven't heard it, it would be dumb to die before you did.
Maybe you'd feel better if you heard it. You haven't visited me
in Texas since my friend Derrick bought his ranch. It's so huge,
like an 80s late night soap opera set, and his girlfriend is so beautiful,
and their dog is so neurotic. And it's all worth seeing, at least once.
You haven't seen it at all, Mom. Mom, the man who loves me
told me he wanted to marry me there. It was at a Halloween party,
and I said, *I can't believe you are telling me this while I'm dressed as a zombie!*
And he laughed, and I laughed, and Mom, you can sit on that bench!
We can sit on it together. What happens if he is telling the truth, Mom?
Don't you think I need you to be alive for that? Mom, you didn't want
to talk on the phone in the hospital, didn't want people to hear you like
that. And now, you have slipped beyond the ability to talk, strapped
to machines like a bomb. Mom, are you listening? All you have to do
is stay. Get through this. There is good food waiting for you, and
fresh laughter, and books. My books even. I mean, what is the point
of writing books if you aren't here to read them. I'm serious. Mom,
please. Stay. Mom. Mom. Please. Stay.

Rabbit Hole

Holding your mother's hand
while she is dying is like trying to love
the very thing that will kill you.

Loving the thing that can kill you
is like hating your fingers
because of how they can feel.

Hating your fingers
because of how they can feel
is like hating the pillowcase
because it smells like her hair.

Hating the pillowcase
is like hating the bed.

Hating the bed
is like hating things
that want to hold you
even as you sob into them.

Hating the things that want to hold you
is like sobering to the fact she will
never hold you again.

Sobering to the fact
she will never hold you again.
is like trying to keep loving
the things you know you can't have.

Loving the things
you know you can't have
is like saying *Goodbye*
and knowing you have to mean it.

Once a fortune cookie told me
that saying *Goodbye* is just a different
way of saying *Hello*.

Once I remembered reading
how *Aloha* is a word meaning
both *hello* and *goodbye*.

Once I remembered reading
how *Aloha* is also a word
which means *peace*.

First Poem After

Please don't hate the dress, blue and white polka dot,
the yellow cardigan, the black flats you thought
would make you so cheerful on the hospital floor.
The brown eyeliner you applied to brighten your eyes,
the brows you drew in like Hepburn would, how
you imagined bursting through your mother's door
like an unexpected bouquet, neither of you could
have known that she'd never regain consciousness.

Don't hate the dress you wore the next day,
burgundy and paired with the same yellow cardigan,
white capris tucked underneath. Another cheerful outfit,
and very you. Your mother always emailed articles
about women wearing dresses with pants, noting,
You always were ahead of the curve.

It was the same outfit you wore last month,
when you performed at the Los Angeles Museum
of Art. It was the outfit you wore on date nights
with the man who loves you. It was the outfit you'd wear
when you watched your mother die, the color draining
from her lips as you held her hand and sobbed.

Don't hate the bra you bought with your mother
three weeks earlier. It is your fault, not the bra's,
that you didn't shower for days, its fabric rubbing
the skin on your ribs raw. You could have removed
it at night, but instead, crawled into the guest bedroom
at your parents' house alone, as you listened
to your father play a voicemail message again
and again and again just to hear your mother's voice.

Don't hate the grey dress you sent your boyfriend
to retrieve from your empty house in Austin.
He brought it to a tailor to sew up its rips
and tears, and to the cleaners, to prepare
for you.

Don't hate the dress, its bright red cardigan,
the boots your mother would have pretended
to hate when she saw them on you at her funeral.
Don't hate the lipstick and the blush that you use
to imitate life on your weary face. Don't hate
the things you put on yourself to get
through this day.

And that night, don't hate your body,
how it responds grateful to your boyfriend's
touch. Don't hate your lips for wanting
to kiss, your fingers for wanting to feel.
Don't hate your lover's arm, which you wear
over you as he sleeps, how his back rises
and falls with each breath, his eyes closed,
his lips, warm and pink with blood.

ONE WEEK AFTER

Before I leave,
my father asks if I want to take
some magazines to read on the flight.

The way he asks, it sounds like a plea,
and I look down, and there is a basket,
overflowing with everything my mom
would have read by now.

My dad is not a reader, and
so all he can do is bring the magazines
where Mom would have seen them,
and leave them there like orphans.

I can't take them all, Pops,
but here... let me...

and I go through the basket
and snip off the address labels,
carefully writing the titles
in the corner, so I can remember.

At home, I begin the process
of changing all the subscriptions
to my Austin address.

Dad said I didn't need to, that
they were likely set to expire anyway,
but he didn't know her like I did:

my mom couldn't resist a bargain,
and when there was a good deal,
she would resubscribe and resubscribe
and resubscribe. Some magazines
were set to keep coming for five years.

And now, they will come to me.

The first one arrived last week,
and I took it out of the mailbox
carefully, a baby bird whom I wanted
to imprint as its new mother.

I opened the pages and wondered
what stories my mom would've loved
best, or ignored entirely, or cut out
and sent to me, or quoted in conversation,
or wondered how it was ever published,

or just read, silently, in the car, in the corner
of the great room, my father in the kitchen,
the sun sliding into the sky's pocket,
my mother in socks with her feet up,
my mother with a magazine in her lap,
my mother with her day wrapping up
my mother finding some peace,
my mother just sitting, just breathing,
my mother just living.

On the Plane Ride Home

Watching the plane's tiny screens,
I get angry at the TV dad who was dying
in the hospital, his lack of machines,
his throat un-punctured with tubes.

My mother was yellow
when I walked into the room,
her body and head swaddled
in blankets and heating pads
since the plasma being pumped
into her body had just been
retrieved from the freezer,
and she needed it faster
than it had time to warm.

I held my mother's hand
over a heating pad, as the machines
all gasped, and wheezed, and groaned
and sucked and sucked and sucked
and sucked and sucked and sucked
and sucked and sucked and sucked

and she never woke up
to give us a speech,
and she never looked
like she was just sleeping,
never opened her eyes
never squeezed my hand back

and the stewardess walks over
and asks if I need anything.
I shake my head *no*, so afraid
I am to open my mouth,
and say anything other
than the truth.

I need my mother.
I need my mother.
I need my mother.

And she didn't make it.

TEXT EXCHANGE WITH OMAR,
WHO ALSO LOST HIS MOM

Can you ask your mom to show
my mom all the cool places in heaven?
My mom has got this obnoxiously
loud laugh tho. Please let your mom
know to skip any quiet, beatific places.
My mom ain't about that afterlife.

There isn't any way to welcome you
to this club everyone becomes a part
of sooner or later

(some too soon)

Man, I wish you were here.

Turn around.

Totally would have been
cool if I was there, right?

[laughing emoji]

[sobbing emoji]

[laughing emoji]

[sobbing emoji]

Two Weeks After

Buying half and half,
and the man behind the counter
is the only person I've seen today.

After I hand him the money,
he asks me how I've been.

Fine, I tell him.

The man behind the counter
has a name tag that reads *Travis*,
and Travis is having trouble
finishing up my purchase.

So… life? he says, not looking
at me. *It's been good?*

Uh-huh, I tell him, looking
at my car in the parking lot,
silently waiting for me.

So everything's good? he says,
as he figures out the problem,
and hits print.

Yes. Very good. Very good,
I say, tucking my unwashed hair
behind an aching ear.

So, things are really great, huh?
he says smiling, finally passing me
the receipt I never wanted.

Yes, I tell Travis, this stranger
to whom I owe nothing
and who doesn't actually care,
I can't complain.

TEXT FROM MY SISTER, JUNE 2015

Definitely have had lots of
sadness lately. The passenger
seatbelt in Dads car smells like
her. But the house is starting to
forget.

THREE WEEKS AFTER

Which stage of grief
is searching the entire internet
for any trace of your dead mother?

Where you Google street-view
her old high school, her childhood home,
the church where your parents were married?

Imagine how surprised I was to find
my mother had started a Twitter account.
She always claimed to be bewildered by it.

But it's true. I found it this morning.
She followed four people:
three of her favorite writers

and me.

One Month After

How deeply and immediately I love
the woman waiting at the elevator bank
of Napperville, Illinois's only Hilton:

her sunburnt legs, her brassy hair cut short,
her peachy pink shorts, her sleeveless white
shirt, her sneakers, her flesh, her warm skin,
her movement, her breath. My brain knows
it is not my mom,

but my body doesn't.

Every muscle of my body aches for her,
to run behind her and lock her in a hug
like I did to my mom. My mother, who
would've feigned to hate it, fuss and pretend
to bite at my arms, and I would get to tease her
about how much she loved me, how much
she loved being hugged by me, and how
I would never ever ever let her go.

I don't move when the elevator doors open.
Instead, I watch this stranger who was no one
to me ascend alone in the hotel's glass elevator,

her heart hidden,
but still beating.

DARK LUCK

I know I'm lucky. I tell people it's a dark luck that I've known
so many people who have lost their mothers. To have friends
who've had to watch their mothers suffer, become pain-riddled,
not recognize their children's faces, who weep and sob for things
that no longer exist: houses that were sold decades earlier, spouses
long dead, dogs turned to sand at the vet. To have friends whose
mothers have died suddenly, without a chance to say goodbye,
without the ability to process, to wrap your head around
the possibility. The phone rings, and the world, as they knew it,
is gone. To have friends whose mothers died while they were still
on bad terms, a wound whose rawness catches every winter wind.
I know people whose mothers died just as they were getting to know
one another, whose mothers never got to know the person they were
destined to become, to be always haunted by what could have been?

Mother, my love, you were a grace that gifted my life. I loved you
every second, and told you and told you and told you. You were there
when I was born, and I was there when you died, released yourself
from a suddenly irreparable body. We spent mother's day weekend
together. I told you my hopes and you celebrated them. You left
having given me a path, your approval, and all the parts of you
I wear like jewelry every day. I wear your wit, your quick loud laugh,
your round Irish cheeks. I wear your face and voice. When I hear
your voice in my head, you tell me to be bold, to be brilliant,
to be the woman you always saw me as.

But it's so hard, Mom,
so hard to be anything
in this life, in this world
that no longer includes
you.

Two Months After

When I wake up, I realize this was the first dream
I had where I knew my mother was dead.

It was not a part of the dream, but I knew, the way
you know things in dreams: that you can float

if you squeeze your eyes shut enough, that this home
that *isn't* your home *is* your home, and, for this dream,

that my mother was dead. I wonder if this is healthy,
a form of acceptance, a good sign.

When I woke after dreams where my mother was alive
again, I didn't know how to feel about it.

But now, even in my dreams, my mother is dead.
There is no sanctuary anymore. Even in my dreams,

I couldn't keep her alive.

There Are Places I'll Remember

Mom always told us she wanted *In My Life*
to play at her funeral. When we removed
the machines from her body, the ones
keeping her alive, I pressed play on my phone
so that it could be the last song she heard,

if she was capable of hearing it. It played
one hundred and forty seven times in a row,
before my brother could finally stop it,
the nurse calling her death moments later.

I untagged it in all devices, not wanting
the song to surprise me while I was driving,
or trying to write, or trying to live, whatever
that even means anymore, now that she is gone.

But the song remains there, airy and beautiful
in my iTunes, in my Top Ten Most Played,
an anchor dragging me back to the bottom.
That moment. That room. The machines

aching in their silence. My mother's labored
breathing. My phone, trying its best, wailing
its song. Our hearts breaking in slow motion,
our hands holding on to whatever still felt warm.

Three Months After

To want to disappear
is different from wanting to die.

To disappear, and to not have
to explain to anyone, to talk to anyone.

To move to somewhere where no one
knows you, where you don't have

to look at a single laughing face.
To elope with this grief,

who is not your enemy, this grief
who maybe now is your best friend.

This grief, who is your husband,
the thing you curl into every night,

falling asleep in its arms, who
wakes up early to make you

your cold thankless breakfast.
To go to that place where

every surface is a blade,
a sharp thing on which to hang

your sorry flesh, to feel something,
anything, other than this.

The First Check Up After My Mother Died

The doctor notices me fidgeting with my ears
like a toddler, and asks if he could look at them.

Yes, I tell him, they had been bothering me,
and I didn't know why.

After the examination, he asks if I had been
through something traumatic recently—

a break-up, or a loss of a job. Yes, I tell him,
not wanting to explain. *How did you know?*

Well, he tells me, *this type of infection is common
among people who have gotten in a pattern*

*of holding back tears. If you don't allow
those tears to drain the way they are supposed to,*

*they stay inside, cause a lot of pain. Do you think
this is what's happening to you?* he asks.

Yes, I nod,
and hold back my tears.

First Book Release After

I arrive in Philadelphia, and my brother has grown a full beard. *It's because of Mom,* he tells me, *When she was alive, I'd always shave before I saw her, because of how much she hated me with facial hair, but now that's she's gone...*

I know what he means.

Dressing for my paperback release, I think about what I can get away with, what my mother won't be there to notice: the unfiled fingernails, the unwashed hair, the stockings with runs. I make my choices, feeling the weight of them: mine.

No one there to notice.

I walk around all day, a dumbass adult, knowing my mother will not be arriving early to swan and beam, to roll her eyes, or pull out a brush, or to call the next day and recount everything.

Things are different, I say to myself,

a thought that felt profound until the moment it hit the air, then it felt dumb. So dumb. Your mother is dead. Of course things are different, and the hopeless wrinkles of your cardigan is the least of it.

But life goes on.

And Mom would have wanted me to go on as well, so my funny-bone heart wanders into the event, wondering the ways my mother's absence will present itself, and wondering what my reaction to it will be.

My father stands alone in the venue, waiting.

Last year, he wore a tux. This year, he wears cargo shorts. *Well...* I think, *this is life after Mom.* My dad sees me, offers a smile that neither of us believes. I walk towards him, and we embrace these lesser versions of each other.

Big night, he says. *Yes,* I agree. And we unload the books in silence.

THE VIEW FROM MY MOTHER'S WINDOW

Tonight a woman came to my reading, and waited until the end
of the signing line before approaching me. She knelt in front
of me, and said, *I knew your mother. We were in a group together.
You know what I mean, right?* And she waited for me to slowly nod,
and I did. She knew you. She knew *you*. She told me how proud you
were of me, how you always talked about me, how all the women
in the group followed the story of my life as a writer, poet, risk-taker,
and now this. *You were clearly her favorite*, she said. And I thanked her.
She said you always teased her at meetings, because she was so flowery
in her descriptions, and you, a gruff Philly broad would say, *Come on,
come on. A tree is just a tree. A sunset is just a sunset. Come on.* But she said
that at your last meeting, you made an announcement, and apologized,
saying you had watched a sunset from your deck, and saw all the different
colors shatter across the water, the glittering strands of light rippling
in every direction. You understood what she meant, finally. You saw it.
I hugged the woman, signed her book, and thanked her for loving you,
for knowing you, for remembering you. I was wearing the same dress
I wore to your funeral. Grey with a black belt, red cardigan, black stockings
and boots. It was an outfit I wore when I toured the previous fall. You were
so proud of me, and I didn't want to drape myself in mourning black.
I wanted to wear the outfit you last saw me in, the one that made you
so proud, the one that reminded me of the book I would never have
written without you. So I wore that dress to your funeral, and promised
myself I would not hate it afterwards so I could keep wearing it
for book events, like tonight, so I can feel you there with me.
When she hugged me, Mom, I hope you felt it. She loved you.
We all did.

Four Months After

I miss the way my mother loved me.
How she saw me as having a place in the world.

My therapist tells me when I speak about my mother,
I use the world *narrative* a lot. It's true.

My mother was my life's narrator.
She told the story of my life to me.

Without her, my life seems so clumsy
and purposeless. Who cares what I do

or don't do? Who cares if I forget,
or remember? This art I create

in the vacuum of her death
feels like so much pale dirt,

weak and heavy and plain.
My mother's love was a bell

that hurts to ring without her.
My life is the static-y remainder

of tape after the beautiful music ends.
How empty and useless the silence,

how I listen with my ear to the speaker
because it's all I have left.

Five Months After

My mom was a big reader of nonfiction, I tell her,
like me. And like you.

She smiles, this mother of a friend, who drove
through the fog of Seattle to pick me up

at the airport and grab a breakfast with me
before my book event that night. *And you see,*

she always used to share with me the books she was
reading. She loved things I didn't love: Hollywood memoirs,

family dynasties, biographies of 1940s socialites. But she knew
what I loved, and she would tell me about books she thought

I should read. The rest of my family aren't readers,
you know? She nods again. *And I know it's weird to ask,*

but I guess what I'm saying is, if you read any books you like,
or think I'd like, could you tell me about them?

Because I don't have that anymore, and I miss it? I say it
like a question, though I know it is the truth.

And she nods, and we both take sips of our coffees,
and I don't remember what the coffee tastes like,

if it's good or bad. I can never remember
if coffee is good or bad, I only remember that I need it.

That it doesn't feel like breakfast without it.
How I pour the cream in every time, and sugar too,

if it needs it, and in this way, I can make even
the most bitter things palatable.

SIX MONTHS AFTER

My therapist tells me it's okay to just cry,
to miss her. Sometimes there is no answer,
no pivoting, no framing things in a better light.

She says it's okay to just miss, to just long,
to look at the world as less than without her,
for now, or forever too. But definitely for now,

it's okay to be buried in it for a bit, to be in it,
to feel it. My mind whirls and buzzes, trying
to find its solution. The insects in the forest

behind my house scream every night trying to find
love in the dark. I sit with my dogs on the porch
when I can't sleep and listen. Together we all watch

the sun creep across the sky like spilled wine.
A new day waiting to flood over us, no matter
how comfortable we've grown with the night.

O LAUGHTER

O, Laughter, you are not forgotten.
   My body is the jam jar you flew into.

You thought it'd be so sweet. You didn't
   realize it was made by crushing the most

gentle of things. O, Laughter, Grief sees
   itself as a knife, carving out what needs

to be seen. See yourself as an ice skater,
   the knives on your feet. Sometimes the pain

bursts out of me like a flock of starlings.
   My throat releases everything but you.

Laughter, be the slyest magician. Make me
   think it's easy work: this levitation.

I'll willingly step into the box, if you'd just
   cut me in half, spin my parts around,

then make me whole again.

FIRST BIRTHDAY AFTER

I would call my mom
as early as possible on my birthday
and she would pretend to forget.

Oh, is today your birthday?
November 26th? Are you sure?

Yes, Mom, I would say.
And she would always say,

Oh yeah, I think I had a little something
to do with that day.

And it was then that I was supposed
to thank her, for giving birth to me
in a hospital proper, and not
on the side of the road.

Thank her for carrying me in her body
for months and eating cottage cheese,
a food she hated, so that fetal me could
develop that smart brain I have now.

And later, to thank her for saving me
from my siblings, who did not like
the new baby, and threw shoes at my crib
in the hopes of silencing my relentless crying,

and oh! Did she mention how much I cried?
I cried and cried and cried until I passed out,
and then I would wake up, and cry some more.

And I could only stop her monologue
by offering the only thing she wanted to hear,
so I always said it, theatrically begrudged, louder
and louder until she could hear it
over her own sweet, ranting voice:

THANK YOU, MOM.

And now it is the morning of my birthday,
and the first one that she is not here to call,

and just to be able to talk to her is the only thing
I want for my birthday, but there aren't enough
candles in the world I could blow out for that magic.

So I'll write it down, at least, get it right on the page
before she would have even been able to say a word:

Thank you, Mom.
Thank you, Mom.
Thank you, Mom.

Thank you.

First Thanksgiving After

In the commercial,
the grandmother wakes up before everyone,
carries her new grandbaby around the house,

and tells the baby that this is Thanksgiving
in her softest, most grandmotherly voice.
Ads like this air every year, and I've always

thought: *This must be tough for people whose mothers
have just died.* And as soon as this thought appears,
I realize this year that person is me,

and I watch the rest of it unfurl,
like a wave you cannot outswim, so you dive
into it because it feels like the safest choice.

In the commercial, the son finally appears
in the doorway. *I'm really glad you are here, Mom,*
he tells her. *Me too,* she replies, *Me too.*

MILE MARKERS

Let this depression smother me under its quilt.
Let this depression lock me in its basement.
Let this depression celebrate its backhand.
Let this depression merge with its river.

Let this future rip my dance card in half.
Let this future spill a drink down my dress.
Let this future try to force eye contact.
Let this future track its mud in my house.

Let the present pull me under like a panicked swimmer.
Let the present rub itself on my gums like cocaine.
Let the present smile wide so I can see the blood in its teeth.
Let the present shut the door til the lock clicks.

SEVEN MONTHS AFTER

Who cares about the wedding, what color the dress, the cake,
the guest list? Who cares about having a baby, the possibility of it,
the joy it promises, it all tastes like sour pennies in my mouth.
Who cares about my hair, my clothing, my shoes, worn and scratched?
Who cares about the thank you cards I keep buying, but never send?
Before my tour last year, I pre-addressed and stamped dozens
of thank you cards for all the bookstore events I had planned,
as my bewildered boyfriend looked on. *Why?* he asked. *It seems like
a lot of work. // It's not work at all,* I told him, *to prepare for gratitude!
// But what if the gig sucks?* he said. *You are not going to want to send
a card then! // Why go into the experience thinking that way,* I told him,
I like going to things expecting the best. // Who would have guessed
you'd be dead nine months later. Something I didn't prepare for.
I haven't sent one thank you note. Not one. They sit useless
in an office I haven't even unpacked. After we got engaged,
I couldn't think of a person I wanted to tell if I couldn't tell you
first. *This is new for me,* I tell my therapist, *to find life so pointless.
I'm usually so grateful. And I am. I am. I am grateful. For so much.
But it's so hard to access. // Be patient,* she tells me. *Everything
you are experiencing is normal.* I nod. And I thank her.
And I pay her. And I leave.

EIGHT MONTHS AFTER

To be motherless
is to fundamentally not belong
to anyone anymore.

I read about how some women
find this freeing; I lost my life's narrator.
My story unraveled at her hospital bed.

In my head, I volunteer for every death:
to give my organs up, leap before a bullet,
to demand to be the sole hostage.

How I want to be seen as brave
for risking what I am happy to give up:
every morning without her; every meal

without her; every moment without her.
This long night of silence from which
I can never wake up.

Nine Months After

In the Q&A, someone asks me
    who is my biggest influence.

My mother is my greatest influence, I say,
    She is the reason I am a writer.

Even nine months after, I can't do it:
    talk about you in the past tense.

I have grown to love performing
    that poem I wrote about you, because

for that moment I can stand in a room full
    of people who don't know you're dead.

Ten Months After

Every night, I read my soon-to-be stepkid to sleep,
like my mom used to do for me. How heavy our eyelids,
how soft the voice floating in the air.

Sometimes she reaches out to hold my hand as I read.
I peek between pages to see if her eyes have closed yet,
if she has let go. Last night, we read

one of her favorites, a story from my childhood,
and I heard my mother's voice rising from my throat,
the soft velvet of it, the rounded corners of the sentences,

softly pulsing the story forward, while guiding the sleeper
to sleep. I smiled thinking of her, this tradition all three
of her children now do with our own,

and I thought, *I wonder who read to her? Who planted
this seed that is still blossoming?* And I realized I'll never know.
My eyes darted to the kid in the bed,

her eyes closed, her breathing slow, as my voice thickened,
tears drifting useless down my face. I miss her. I miss her.
I miss her. I keep reading until the story ends.

The kid is asleep, I think. But still, I sit silent
in that room, waiting until the very moment
I'm sure it will be okay to leave her.

ON TURTLES

My mother began wearing turtles shortly after beginning therapy.
Turtles, she explained to me years ago, symbolize this new period
for her. Turtles are slow. When scared, they retreat into themselves,
knowing they can stay there for as long as they need. But when it is
time, turtles slowly pull their heads out, poke out their stubby legs,
and move forward. For years afterwards, every birthday, Christmas,
would mean a gift box from me full of turtle jewelry: pins mostly,
gaudy or subtle, silver or gold, vintage or new, always cheap though.
We lost things all the time, she and I. Nothing made us retreat
into our shells more quickly than our stupidity costing someone else
good money. When she died, my dad gifted it all back to me, arriving
in a box with my mother's old sweaters. My fiancé walks in on me
breathing in their smell. The turtles were old, mostly broken, missing
gems, their pins bent, their legs and heads snapped off. But mom
kept them, and so do I, the misfit family of them, living in my office,
alongside a slim book my father also sent along. It was a gratitude
journal my mother began keeping, never imagining that she'd be dead
within the month. It took nearly a year for me to open it. When I did,
I saw every entry was about me.

Eleven Months After

This has been a year of last times,
most of which were planned, but not all.

I have earned my PhD in goodbyes.
In the weeks after my mother died,

I lay in my twin bed and watched
documentaries about dead mothers,

movies about dead mothers, read books
about dead mothers, slept. *You should be*

writing about this, I remember constantly
thinking like a reflex.

NO! I'd spit back at myself.
The idea of it. The normalcy of it.

Why would I want to remember this time?
The shotgun blast that grief exploded through

my everything? But it didn't matter.
I still found myself here, writing. Sometimes

it was just *my mother is dead my mother is dead*
my mother is dead again and again,

hoping that in writing it down, it would
start to make sense. Before, I used writing

to remember things. Now I write to just
get these thoughts out of my head.

So if you wanted a poem, there it is.
my mother is dead my mother is dead

my mother is dead. She'll never read it.
So honestly, who cares?

ALSO NOT A METAPHOR

There is a blank page
in my journal.

It was an accident.

I apologize
to the emptiness.

I tell it,

*There should have been
a poem here.*

It doesn't say anything back.

LATE MAY

Ever since my mom died
I've been dreading Mother's Day,
I tell him, *but now that*
I am here, I feel like...

MOTHER'S DAY TEXT EXCHANGE WITH OMAR, WHO ALSO LOST HIS MOM

So grateful your mother gave us you.
Thinking of you on this shitty ass Day

Trying to Hug a Field Day

[heart emoji]
[heart emoji]
[heart emoji]
[heart emoji]
[heart emoji]
[heart emoji]
[heart emoji]
[heart emoji]
[heart emoji]
[heart emoji]
[heart emoji]
[heart emoji]
[heart emoji]
[heart emoji]
[heart emoji]
[heart emoji]
[heart emoji]
[heart emoji]
[heart emoji]
[heart emoji]
[heart emoji]
[heart emoji]
[heart emoji]
[heart emoji]
[heart emoji]
[heart emoji]
[heart emoji]
[heart emoji]
[heart emoji]
[heart emoji]
[heart emoji]
[heart emoji]

The Morning After Mother's Day

We make love with the windows open
as it was cool last night for May in Texas.
We hear the car doors of our neighbors
open and slam as we keep our voices low.
Afterwards, the lawn floods with cardinals:
bright red males and soft yellow females,
hopping from branch to grass to branch.
From my office window I watch them,
just past the pictures lining the sill: you,
and your daughter, and me and my mother,
the necklace you gave me, the framed valentine,
the booklet I bought years earlier, never imagining
what was to come: *Preparing for Marriage.*

ON THE FIRST ANNIVERSARY
OF MY MOTHER'S DEATH

Grief, the kind that terrorizes, is like the squirrels who steal
from the bird feeders we put on the deck in almost zero ways,
except in how I hate them. Although the squirrels are doing
exactly what squirrels do. Don't squirrels need to eat too?
Why are birds more important to feed than squirrels? Birds
can fly! & doesn't grief over my dead mother deserve to be
felt, to grip my body in its fist and squeeze? For the squirrels,
I take my smallest dog, shove him through the doggie door,
his head pointed toward the feeder, and he takes off, barking,
the hair on his back raised like a wave. And the birds return:
blue jays and cardinals, titmouses and warblers, the white-winged
doves which only began to appear recently and seem kind of like
assholes, scaring off the smaller birds as they dig for sunflower
seeds. *Those pigeons are mean*, my soon-to-be stepdaughter says.
They're doves, I say, as if that makes a difference. My mother
would've loved the deck, its wildlife, this kid in my life
who loves me. *I want to make a joke about you*, she said yesterday,
*but I need you to spell your name on a piece of paper and also give me a list
of all the presidents.* Mom would've loved that. I tell my fiancé
that I feel closest to my mom when I'm with his daughter,
the things I share with her—stories, and inside jokes,
and perspectives, and speculations, and gifts, and hugs,
and food, and cooking, and the *everything everything everything*.
But sometimes, that happiness feels like betrayal. *Every day I don't fall
on the ground and sob about her feels like disrespect*, I tell him, *to what
she meant to me. What I lost.* The dogs are sent to the groomers
for the day, and all day, I watch squirrels march up to the feeder
and take what they think is theirs: those oily black seeds.
Their tails flick as they crack the shells and eat the soft insides.
I rap on the windows, open the door, and shout, but they only
turn, knowing I am unwilling to put in the effort to step outside.
By nightfall, the feeder is empty. The squirrels hop through
the grass in the rain to see if they missed anything. The lights
shut out, and I am alone. *Mom*, I say to the rain, *I miss you.*
I can feel her rolling her eyes in heaven, something she'd do

when she felt something, but knew it would be corny
to acknowledge it. We were a conspiracy, you and I, Mom.
I miss all the ways you saw me. The way you'd probably laugh
at me, crying in a dark house, so angry at squirrels, but how
you'd circle back, eventually giving me the comfort I wanted.
It was never about the squirrels. I miss crying into the couch
cushions of your laugh. How light you made everything.
How heavy everything is now that you are gone.

June Wedding

The florist wrapped my bridal bouquet
with the lace from your wedding gown.
I squeezed it as dad walked me down the aisle.

The wedding portrait of you two sat framed
on the boat's hull, next to the wedding portrait
of my now-husband's parents, also deceased.

There were so many ghosts to invite to this wedding,
we decided to have it on a boat. The sun could shine
wherever it wanted. Everything was filled with light.

After the ceremony, my best friend evoked your name.
Raising her glass into the air, she said she could feel
how happy you must be right now.

My husband smiled at me, as my now-stepdaughter
reached up to touch my face. I looked at her.
Happy tears, yes? she asked, cupping my cheeks.

Yes, I tell her, and mean it. I kiss her, and then him.
Behind this sea of family and friends, I see the light:
how it bounces off the water and races towards us,

how it ripples boundless, like electricity, like joy,
like your laughter, irresistible and bright,
an impossible thing to contain.

POEMS THAT WENT NOWHERE

The little confectionary she would make for St. Patty's day: sugar, butter, cream cheese rolled into balls and dipped into cinnamon. *Irish Potatoes.* How sweet they were. The sacks I brought to my teachers, the smell of it, of her, everywhere.

Her as a teenager, protesting in front of the supermarket she worked at. Hand-painted signs insisting everyone should *Boycott Grapes!* How confused the old people in her neighborhood were: *But isn't that the nice girl who works in the deli?* as Mom passed out pamphlets filled with the words of César Chávez.

How she would pray to just one saint: Saint Lawrence Justinian. Other people in our neighborhood prayed to St. Jude when they lost things, or St. Christopher when they were traveling, to the Virgin Mary to protect their children. No. Mom prayed only to Saint Lawrence Justinian. She thought the more popular saints got prayers all the time, so she chose a saint no one had heard of, so he'd be available, and hopefully eager to make her miracles come true.

How even now, when I find myself in a hotel room, I want to call her to tell her how fancy it is. How I still ask for posters and fliers for my events, as if she was still collecting them. How I don't know what to do with it all. How worthless it has become.

How my mother's last voicemail to me was about how proud she was of me, and how I needed to sign extra bookplates for her, and how she ended it by saying *I love you,* which she never said because she felt like if you say it all the time it loses meaning.

How she said I love you,
and I have it recorded.

How I do not listen to it.
How I know it's there.

ROLL CALL

Dorothy Parker once said,
   Women and elephants,
   we never forget.

And Gwendolyn Brooks said,
   I've stayed in the front yard all my life.
   I want a peek at the back.

And Emily Dickinson said,
   I am nobody
   Who are you?

And Sylvia Plath said,
   Love, it gets you going
   like a fat gold watch.

And Lucille Clifton said,
   These hips are big hips
   they need space to move around in.

And Sharon Olds said,
   Do what you are going to do
   and I'll tell about it.

And Anne Sexton said,
   Men kill for this, or for as much.
   But what of the dead?

And Mary Oliver said,
   I don't want to end up
   simply having visited this world.

And weeks before she died at the age of 43,
Gabrielle Boulaine shouted from a stage,
   Take it from a girl who's already half angel:
   Do not wait.

And I remember saying into the phone,
I remember saying:
    Ma, it's hard sometimes
    to know if you're making
    any difference
    at all.

And my mom said,
    Baby, don't you realize how lucky you are?
    They used to burn women like you.

She said,
    You got a voice, right?
    Well then. *Use it.*

SLEEPING IN LATE WITH MY MOTHER

She apologizes. It's not like her. She's usually up by six.
But it's the weekend, you tell her, *there is no need to rush!*

The plan for the day is breakfast somewhere and walking
somewhere else. I'm happy, but Mom can't believe that

she forgot to bring conditioner, or that she slept so late.
The housekeeper at the discount hotel knocks. *We're still here,*

we're still here! she shouts back. Girls' weekend, just us two,
and still we have to remind each other it's okay to take our time.

No rush, we say to each other, firmly. I'm writing two poems
a day all summer: one every morning and again every night.

It is morning and my mom tells me, *Write a poem about this,*
but don't mention I slept in so late! Just put down that your mother

is taking it easy, that your mother is taking her time for once! So I do
what she says, sort of. And the housekeeper knocks again.

But this time, my mother doesn't jump. Instead, she leans back,
comfortable, and shouts: *Still here, Still here! We are still here!*

ACKNOWLEDGEMENTS

Grateful acknowledgements are given to the following organizations whose support was absolutely instrumental in the creation of this book:

the **National Endowment for the Arts** for granting me a NEA Literature Fellowship in Poetry;

the **University of Pennsylvania** and the **Kelly Writers House** for naming me their 2010-2011 ArtsEdge Writer-in-Residence;

and the **Berkshire Taconic Community Foundation** for naming me their 2013 Amy Clampitt House Writer-in-Residence.

Grateful acknowledgements also are made to the following literary journals, in which some of these writings first appeared in slightly different forms:

Drunk in a Midnight Choir – "Money," "On Turtles," and "Seven Months After"
Harpoon Review – "Two Months After," "Four Months After," and "Six Months After"
Lunch Ticket – "First Check-up After"
SUSAN: The Journal – "Dark Luck," "Five Months After," and "Eleven Months After"
Wildness – "The View from My Mother's Window"

NOTES

"MY MOTHER DOES NOT GIVE ADVICE": As noted in the poem, all the quotes where given to me as-is by my mother, and this represents my best efforts to properly cite them. The quote which opens this poem appears most often in psychology and counseling books and websites, where it is attributed to either the Tao Te Ching or as being a phrase from Taoist philosophy, although the translator and/or a direct book citation is unknown. The quote which begins "Never fear shadows…" is attributed to Ruth E. Renkel, but I was unable to track down from which book or speech it originates. The quote that ends the poem was misattributed by my mother (and numerous others) to poet/playwright Guillaume Apollinaire; it was actually written by poet Christopher Logue, and used in posters advertising an Apollinaire exhibition, which accounts for the widespread misattribution.

"ELEVEN MONTHS AFTER": As noted in this poem, after my mother's passing I filled my house with books that helped me feel less alone in my grief. Here is a list of the ones I returned to most often: the poetry collections *Dear Darkness* (Knopf, 2010) and *The Book of Hours* (Knopf, 2014) by Kevin Young, as well as his incredible and necessary anthology *The Art of Losing: Poems of Grief and Healing* (Bloomsbury, 2013); *The Year of Magical Thinking* (Vintage, 2007) by Joan Didion; *A Grief Observed* (HarperOne, 2001) by C.S. Lewis; *Motherless Daughters: The Legacy of Loss* (Da Capo Lifelong Books, 2014); *I Love Science* (Write Bloody Publishing, 2012); *Ceremony for the Choking Ghost* (Write Bloody Publishing, 2010) by Karen Finneyfrock; and *Vintage Sadness* (Big Lucks, 2017) by Hanif Abdurraqib.

"ROLL CALL": The Dorothy Parker quote is from her poem "Ballade of Unfortunate Mammals" which can be found in her book *Death and Taxes* (1931). The Gwendolyn Brooks quote is from her poem "a song in the front yard" which can be found in her book *Selected Poems* (1963). The Emily Dickinson quote is from her poem "I'm nobody! Who are You?" which can be found in her book *The Poems of Emily Dickinson* (1951). The Sylvia Plath quote is from her poem "Morning Song" which can be found in her book *Ariel* (1966). The Lucille Clifton quote is from her poem "homage to my hips" which can be found in her book *Good Woman* (1987). The Sharon Olds quote is from her poem "I Go Back to May 1937" which can be found in her book *Strike Sparks: Selected Poems 1980-2002* (2004). The Anne Sexton quote is from her poem "The Truth the Dead Know" which can be found in her book *The Complete Poems* (1981). The Mary Oliver quote is from her poem "When Death Comes" which can be found in her book *New and Selected Poems, Volume One* (2005). The Gabrielle Boulaine quote comes from her poem "Life Sentence," which can be found in the permanent collection of the Performance Poetry Preservation Project poetry slam archive housed at the Rauner Special Collections Library of Dartmouth College.

ABOUT THE AUTHOR

Photo by Anis Mojgani

CRISTIN O'KEEFE APTOWICZ is the author of six previous books of poetry—*Dear Future Boyfriend*; *Hot Teen Slut*; *Working Class Represent*; *Oh, Terrible Youth*; *Everything is Everything* and *The Year of No Mistakes*—which are all currently available through Write Bloody Publishing. Her second collection of poetry, *Hot Teen Slut*, was recently optioned for a film adaption, and her sixth collection of poetry, *The Year of No Mistakes*, was named the Book of the Year for Poetry by the Writers' League of Texas. Aptowicz is also the author of two nonfiction books: *Words In Your Face: A Guided Tour Through Twenty Years of the New York City Poetry Slam* (Soft Skull Press), which U.S. Poet Laureate Billy Collins wrote "leaves no doubt that the slam poetry scene has achieved legitimacy and taken its rightful place on the map of contemporary literature"; and *Dr. Mütter's Marvels: A True Tale of Intrigue and Innovation at the Dawn of Modern Medicine* (Avery Books/Penguin), which spent three months on the *New York Times* Best Seller list. Recent awards include a National Endowment for the Arts Fellowship in Literature, the ArtsEDGE Writer-in-Residence position at the University of Pennsylvania, and the Amy Clampitt House Residency. When not on tour, Aptowicz lives and writes in Austin, TX, with her husband, the novelist/screenwriter Ernest Cline, and their family.

For more information, including upcoming tour dates, please visit her website at:

www.aptowicz.com

If You Like Cristin O'Keefe Aptowicz, Cristin O'Keefe Aptowicz Likes...

I Love Science by Shanny Jean Maney

Uh-Oh by Derrick C. Brown

Pecking Order by Nicole Homer

The Pocketknife Bible by Anis Mojgani

Said the Manic to the Muse by Jeanann Verlee

Bouquet of Red Flags by Taylor Mali

Courage: Daring Poems for Gutsy Girls (Anthology) edited by
Karen Finneyfrock, Mindy Netifee, and Rachel McKibbens

Write Bloody Publishing distributes and promotes great books of fiction, poetry and art every year. We are an independent press dedicated to quality literature and book design, with an office in Los Angeles, CA.

Our employees are authors and artists so we call ourselves a family. Our design team comes from all over America: modern painters, photographers and rock album designers create book covers we're proud to be judged by.

We publish and promote 8-12 tour-savvy authors per year. We are grass-roots, D.I.Y., bootstrap believers. Pull up a good book and join the family. Support independent authors, artists and presses.

**Want to know more about Write Bloody books, authors and events?
Join our maling list at**

www.writebloody.com

IF YOU LIKE *HOW TO LOVE THE EMPTY AIR* CHECK OUT CRISTIN O'KEEFE APTOWICZ'S OTHER BOOKS...

Dear Future Boyfriend
In her quirky debut volume, Cristin O'Keefe Aptowicz tackles love ("Science"), heartbreak ("Lit"), and thieving suburban punks ("Ode to the Person Who Stole My Family's Lawn Gnome"), among other hilariously idiosyncratic topics.

Hot Teen Slut
In her second collection of poetry, Cristin O'Keefe Aptowicz serves up a memoir-in-verse about her first job out of college: writing and editing for porn. Aptowicz dramatizes the hopes, humor and ambitions of a young poet's first steps into a very surreal "real world."

Working Class Represent
In her third collection of poetry, Cristin O'Keefe Aptowicz celebrates the ups and downs of being a performance poet with a day job. This book continues Aptowicz's tradition of witty, honest, and wildly original work.

Oh, Terrible Youth
In her fourth collection of poetry, Cristin O'Keefe Aptowicz uses her youth as a muse. This plump collection commiserates and celebrates all the wonder, terror, banality, and comedy that is the long journey through to adulthood.

Everything is Everything
In her fifth collection of poetry, Cristin O'Keefe Aptowicz polishes her obsessions until they gleam. *Everything is Everything* illuminates the dark corners of the curiosity cabinet, shining the light on everything that is utterly strange, wonderfully absurd and 100% true.

The Year of No Mistakes
In her sixth collection of poetry, Cristin O'Keefe Aptowicz bears witness to the unraveling of a decade-long relationship. Intimate, observant, and unflinchingly honest, Aptowicz explores love, nostalgia, grief, desire, envy, and hope in poems that showcase her emblematic funny and heartbreaking style.

ALL BOOKS ARE AVAILABLE ON WRITE BLOODY PUBLISHING

America's Independent Press

WRITE BLOODY BOOKS

After the Witch Hunt — Megan Falley

Aim for the Head, Zombie Anthology — Rob Sturma, Editor

Amulet — Jason Bayani

Any Psalm You Want — Khary Jackson

Birthday Girl with Possum — Brendan Constantine

The Bones Below — Sierra DeMulder

Born in the Year of the Butterfly Knife — Derrick C. Brown

Bouquet of Red Flags — Taylor Mali

Bring Down the Chandeliers — Tara Hardy

Ceremony for the Choking Ghost — Karen Finneyfrock

Clear Out the Static in Your Attic — Rebecca Bridge & Isla McKetta

Counting Descent — Clint Smith

Courage: Daring Poems for Gutsy Girls — Karen Finneyfrock, Mindy Nettifee
& Rachel McKibbens, Editors

Dear Future Boyfriend — Cristin O'Keefe Aptowicz

Do Not Bring Him Water — Caitlin Scarano

Drunks and Other Poems of Recovery — Jack McCarthy

The Elephant Engine High Dive Revival Anthology

Everyone I Love Is a Stranger to Someone Else — Annelyse Gelman

Everything is Everything — Cristin O'Keefe Aptowicz

Favorite Daughter — Nancy Huang

The Feather Room — Anis Mojgani

Floating, Brilliant, Gone — Franny Choi

Glitter in the Blood: A Guide to Braver Writing — Mindy Nettifee

Good Grief — Stevie Edwards

The Good Things About America — Derrick Brown and Kevin Staniec, Editors

The Heart of a Comet — Pages D. Matam

Hello. It Doesn't Matter. — Derrick C. Brown

Hot Teen Slut — Cristin O'Keefe Aptowicz

CPSIA information can be obtained
at www.ICGtesting.com
Printed in the USA
FSHW04n2133050418
46387FS